Teeth Matters

&

Other Life

Lessons

Denora E. Watts

Front cover art by Ana Latese, Illustrator & Designer: www.anaLatese.com

ISBN: 978-0-359-85576-6

PublishNation LLC
www.publishnation.net

Acknowledgements

Believing in one's self is the hardest
thing to do. All my love and gratitude
to my parents Robert H. Watts, Sr. and
Dorothy M. Tyler, who believed in me
when I could not figure out how to
believe in myself. You will always be
so special to me.

I thank all of you who never stop
believing me.
You know who you are

I

You

To my daughters Ashlynn Elyse,
Dominique Karesee
&
my Grandbaby Aliyah Elyse

"Never, Never Ever quit…"
                    -Winston Churchill.

Teeth matter... teeth will always

matter.

Pearly white teeth send a

message of confidence,

happiness and success

Bad teeth are a distraction
mentally and physically and
create pause for question and
judgement.

Always look for the good in

others ... it gives you peace.

Identify and accept your role in the problem. it should provide clarity.

Be Prepared for the impact that

your words and actions may

have on others.

Never Apologize for acts of

kindness.

Reckless Words are not easily

forgotten.

Your Voice does Matter.

The Tone of your voice drives the

outcome of the conversation.

Teach People how to treat you.

Know the difference between eye

contact and staring.

Silence speaks volumes

Always believe in your ability to see the task through. Don't be afraid of what awaits you at the end.

Truly You are the star of your own play.

Cheer for yourself then take a

bow.

Avoid eyes that don't smile.

Advocate for the little person. It's

good for your spirit.

You must advocate for your

child's success. our future

depends on it

Time shows no mercy to

anyone... stay busy

Feeling lost can be temporary ...

ask questions, ask for help

Look for Daily lessons in life

Cleanse your spirit ...remove

toxic people from your life

Define Toxic people...people who
don't pore positivity into your
life ever

Feel the moment... Seize the

opportunity.

Start with yourself in your

search for the answer to the

problem

Self-reflect every day.

Everyday gets better. Today is
better than yesterday, and
tomorrow will be better than
today.

Celebrate your day... your born day. This birthday could be your last.

Set Your time frames ... be

ready to change your time

frames.

Friendships need nurturing lest

they die.

Plan A didn't work. Plan B is to

go back and make Plan A work.

Your actions are verification of

your word.

Understand what "Word is

Bond" means.

Cry for people you don't know...

it keeps you human.

Children are little people Treat

them with Respect.

Your children reflect you, and
all you poured into them or not.

Girlfriend don't forget your girl
when you get a man. You will
need her again someday.

Do not take your friends for
granted as you get older, they
will be more precious than gold.

Forget about the one that got away. Consider it was fate, or destined for a different place and time.

Real love transcends time and

distance. True love no know

ends or boundaries.

Everything is a matter of time.

Time does not heal all wounds it

just soothes the memories.

Eventually over time you will

forget.

Find a way to tell the truth

Live in your truth... it will free

you from guilt.

People respect the truth, Want the truth but often can't handle or respect the truth. Give it to them anyway.

Respect never gets old.

Set your ex-love free
emotionally. Tell them to Move
on, and you do the same.

Walk away, set yourself free.

Three minutes of Fame can

change your life

A little pressure creates new

productivity.

Live in the moment. Tomorrow

may never come.

Bet on You.

I bring me.

Boyfriends or dates are not valid

reasons to miss family

milestone celebrations.

Simulation is the greatest for of

admiration

Expect nothing and that way

you be surprised.

Stop making excuses for being a

no show. Prioritize your life.

Fill in the gaps where needed.

Your birthday is the only day

that belongs to you Celebrate!

lovers Set your Ex Free. its your

love that is holding hostage.

Clean out the kitchen before you

bring in a new chief.

What you do speaks so loudly

no one hears a word you are

saying.

Focus on moving forward not what stopped you from moving.

Demand that people speak to you with respect, and kindness. If you don't it will wear down your confidence.

Smoking really causes bad breath that no mint can ever mask.

Don't Smoke... sounds corny

but it ruins your teeth.

Teeth Matter because broken or

missing teeth breed judgements

Ten shots of Tequila are far too

many FYI

Follow your Gut it is about

%100. Accurate.

Any age Teeth matter, mostly

because we need them to

masticate.

Long distance love must be short term.

Speak your positivity into the

atmosphere...it will come back to

you.

Success is the best Revenge.

IF you are leader ... lead stop half

stepping.

Lead by example

Don't ask other to do what you

would not do.

If you are a leader your teeth

matter

Know what kind of leader you

are... people are depending on it.

Say Good morning, Good Morning when you walk into work... positive energy is contagious.

Exercise and Understand the

power of Silence

Be fair, consistent and firm.

these are great qualities of a

Leader

Listen more that you talk, and don't cut people off mid-sentence.

Where are the people that voted

for Donald Trump?

Who will admit that they voted

for Donald Trump?

Embrace Change... Don't deny it.

IF it is broke...throw it out Don't
try to fix it.

Self-Preservation is a must.

Nothing is as good as the first

time.

Remember the first time, you

need something to compare.

Create memories in all you do.

One day your memories will be

stories.

Choose your words wisely you do

not have to respond

immediately.

Weight is not an image, but not

a state of mind.

Learn a new word once a day or

make it once a week.

Random acts of Kindness are

contagious.

A little Laughter goes a long

way.

Learn to laugh at yourself.

Learn to Really listen ... stop

Talking. just listen.

People are like shoes... don't force

the fit.

There is a reason for the season,

What makes sense now may

appear Nonsense next season.

Cutting Some one-off mid-

Sentence …that's not listening.

Good Wine, Good friends equals

the Best of times.

Be the one that knows the wine.

Do Not show up to any invite

empty handed.

Wine grows fine over time.

Wine is the beginning of a great

conversation.

Do let the Wine be the reason.

Good Wine Cleanses the palate

in more ways than one.

Pray for all People

Take a Social Media Fast.

Laugh at yourself often.

Don't lie to yourself. It creates

delusions.

Pray short prayers everyday.

God is Real .... Believe it.

Pray for all people.

You set the tone for Success or

Failure.

Send the representative only

when necessary.

Trust yourself first.

Bet on You again.

The rules of the game are not the

same for everyone.

Find out why It is true...don't

hate the game... hate the player.

The beginning of the end is

always right in front of you.

Your smile lights up the room.

"To your own self be true". learn

what that means.

Start slow with the long deep

smile... watch the response

Writers Read-Readers Write.

Missing Teeth are a distraction.

Welcome to New York--- really

its invitation only.

New York is not for everyone.

Love New York or Hate New York

there is not in between.

New York has its own energy

and a unique smell.

New York City is a feeling... It

hits you as soon as you land, by

car, train, or plane.

New Yorkers are Survivors.

I

♥

New York.

Today, Tomorrow, Forever.

The Best Smell is the Morning

Coffee

The most precious words on the

phone "Hello Mom" "Hi Mommy'

Live your life with the Audacity

of Hope

Some things you must do for

yourself.

Past lovers leave Imprints on our

Hearts

Never Forgotten... The ones we

loved

The spark of a true love ignites

an internal flame.

Fear kills Dreams

Fear immobilizes productivity.

Success leaves Clues.

Listen to the lyrics of music.

you will be moved

There is a song for every season

Music will take you back and allow you to live the moment all over again.

Dogs are smarter than we think

Live in the moment. Savor it.

Time changes your mind.

Admit you miss him/her.

You know you want to ask

someone" what happened to your

teeth?"

Learn the art of wine
appreciation it makes life so
much better.

Feet matter too.

Dream Big sounds simple but it

works.

Love hard, Love often, Love

without regrets.

Silence is beyond Golden it's a

must.

Budget Time Wisely, you can't

get back one moment in time.

Know when the end is the end.

Leave before you are asked to

leave

Transparency means

Vulnerability.

Don't cry Fake tears.

Let yourself be moved by tears...

its part of being human.

Don't fake orgasms.

Send the flowers Now.

Define your Boundaries

Don't let anyone cross your

boundaries.

President Obama is sorely

missed.

Was it all a dream?

Sisters are magical.

Don't waste your time

complaining.

Take negative energy to drive

you to a positive place.

Sit and think and Think and

sit. then create movement

Always consider the source.

Whose report are you going to

believe?

IF you don't love your Job find

another one.

Be the example of work place

expectations.

Don't' overshare in your

professional setting.

Don't over dress for work, don't

under dress for work.

Stop complaining it clouds your

Reality

Don't talk about it - be about it.

Let your voice be heard

Thank God for everything, every day. all day.

Keep it simple say:" To God be

the glory"

Check in on the old people

Love as hard as you can forget
protecting your heart. Your
brain will catch you if fall. Go
for it!

You are your own celebrity.
That's Right you are a
celebrity... go ahead dodge the
poparatzi.

Get out of your own Way.

Mutual Respect Never grows old.

Try using a soft tone, when

speaking...it relaxes people.

Cut people off who cut you off.

Wake up! Don't sleep the day away.

Do NOT send the representative.

Life is too short to drink cheap

wine.

Wine deserves elegant glasses.

Learn how to think…. it's

important.

Understand how to give and

receive feedback.

Pause when asked a question. it

buys time to respond correctly.

SPA the day away- it refreshes

you.

Be a mentor to someone, you are

wiser than you think

Have a mentor, you
(unfortunately) are not the
smartest one in the room.

If you are the smartest one in the room.... Find a new room. You need new challenges

At every age, in every stage of

life- Show respect.

Let the Sunshine Warm your face- it feels good and it's a great source of vitamin D

Have a "that's my song."

Start your day with a song. It sets the tone for a happy Day.

Don't rush your song... learn the

lyrics.

Spend a day playing all "your

songs"

Don't waste your time on people who don't listen to you when you speak.

Make a personal disclaimer.

Looking at your phone

repeatedly will force me to walk

away. -

Demand Absolutely NO Phones

at the dinner table, any

meetings, church and in the bed.

Model the respect you want.

"Look at yourself and say "self?"

Self will say "Yes"

Is it as good as the first time?

Say less, Listen More

Tone Matters

Its is never too late to realize

your dream;

Close your eyes, sit and be still

your dreams will come to you.

IF you want to write a book.
Make time to write one word at a
time One word will turn into one
sentence, one sentance will turn
into one paragraph and before
you know you will have finished
your book.